How to Take the ACHE Out of Mistakes

Kimberly Feltes Taylor & Eric Braun

Illustrated by St

free spirit
PUBLISHING®

Text copyright © 2019 by Kimberly Feltes Taylor and Eric Braun
Illustrations copyright © 2019 by Free Spirit Publishing Inc.

Library of Congress Cataloging-in-Publication Data
Names: Feltes Taylor, Kimberly, author. | Braun, Eric, 1971– author. | Mark, Steve, illustrator.
Title: How to take the ache out of mistakes / Kimberly Feltes Taylor and Eric Braun ; illustrated by Steve Mark.
Description: Minneapolis, MN : Free Spirit Publishing Inc., [2019] | Series: Laugh & learn series | Audience: 008–013. | Includes index.
Identifiers: LCCN 2018029816 (print) | LCCN 2018035444 (ebook) | ISBN 9781631983092 (Web PDF) | ISBN 9781631983108 (ePub) | ISBN 9781631983085 (paperback) | ISBN 1631983083 (paperback)
Subjects: LCSH: Failure (Psychology) in children—Juvenile literature. | Self-acceptance—Juvenile literature.
Classification: LCC BF723.F27 (ebook) | LCC BF723.F27 F45 2019 (print) | DDC 158.1—dc23
LC record available at https://lccn.loc.gov/2018029 816

Reading Level Grade 5; Interest Level Ages 8–13;
Fountas & Pinnell Guided Reading Level V

Cover and interior design by Emily Dyer and Shannon Pourciau
Edited by Brian Farrey-Latz

10 9 8 7 6 5 4 3 2 1
Printed in the United States of America
V20300319

Free Spirit Publishing Inc.
6325 Sandburg Road, Suite 100
Minneapolis, MN 55427–3674
(612) 338-2068
help4kids@freespirit.com
www.freespirit.com

FSC
www.fsc.org
MIX
Paper from
responsible sources
FSC® C005010

Dedication

To the young people in my life who have trusted me to help guide them when they've made mistakes. And to my husband, Chris Taylor, for his endless love and support.
—KFT

For Henry and Fergus, whose abilities to grow from mistakes consistently inspire me.
—EB

Acknowledgments

Special thanks to Marjorie Lisovskis for believing in this book when it was just a tiny idea. A big thank you also to Brian Farrey-Latz, our editor, for his excellent guidance in bringing the book to life. Many thanks as well to everyone at Free Spirit Publishing for all their work on our book. Finally, thank you to Thomas S. Greenspon, Ph.D., whose books on perfectionism were an invaluable resource.

Contents

Introduction: You Must Be Mistaken

You've probably heard people say, "Everyone makes mistakes."

And it's true—*everyone* makes mistakes. Your mom makes mistakes. So does your dad. And your teacher. Your principal, best friend, cousin, neighbor, Great Aunt Tutu, and your favorite sports stars and singers. The most popular internet video star of all time, the most famous movie stars, and every politician ever. (*Especially* them.)

So what's the big deal? If everyone makes mistakes, why do you need a book to learn about them?

Because not everyone knows how to handle mistakes. People might deny they made a mistake, or avoid thinking about it, or lash out at others, or get really mad at themselves.

Because sometimes small mistakes can lead to bigger mistakes. And big problems. If we don't learn from our mistakes we miss a chance to do better.

Because sometimes making mistakes can leave you feeling embarrassed or all alone—like you're the only one who would do something so "stupid."

Because for some people, WORRYING about making a mistake is a real problem. They stress about being wrong. They get so wound up with worry they never try anything new because they don't want to mess up.

Sometimes making a mistake can give you a sick, twisty feeling in your stomach.

This book helps you take the ACHE out of mistakes.

Mistakes come in all shapes and sizes, just like the people who make them. Some mistakes are small, like tripping over your own feet. Some mistakes are a little more important, like forgetting to walk the dog or ignoring a big school project because you just don't want to face it.

Mistakes can be accidents, like striking out in softball or getting a problem wrong on a math test. But did you know that sometimes people *decide* to make mistakes?

It's true. They might lie to a parent,* cheat on a test, or steal from a friend or a store. Their mistake was *choosing* to be dishonest. If they keep choosing to be dishonest, their behavior becomes more than a mistake. It becomes part of who they are.

Sometimes when people make a mistake, all they want to do is get away—from the mistake and from everyone around them. However, hiding is *not* the thing to do. Instead, you can deal with your mistake in a way that helps you. You have the power to move on in a healthy way.

IMPORTANT NOTE: This book will *not* teach you how to *never* make a mistake again. That's impossible. It *will* teach you how to own your mistakes. It will help you fix them. It will also show you how to learn from them. And once you start owning, fixing, and learning from your mistakes, you'll feel smart, mature, and independent. Because you ARE smart, mature, and independent. Others will see you that way too—no mistake about it.

*When you see *parent* or *parents* in this book, think of the person or people who are raising you or who take care of you. That may be your mom or dad or another adult like a foster parent, a grandparent, an aunt or uncle—or whoever is most responsible for you.

Chapter 1

How It Feels to Make a Mistake

Uh-oh, you blew it. You stumbled, bumbled, or fumbled. You messed up. You **really** messed up. Or maybe you just, you know, *kind of* messed up. Maybe no one will notice. Or maybe it's too late—everyone noticed.

Whether your mistake was big, small, or in between, it might not feel good. It might even feel really bad. Or you might be okay with making a mistake, knowing that it just means you're human. Most kids have a lot of different thoughts after making a mistake. Screwing up might lead you to think some of these thoughts:

I don't care, I didn't want to do that anyway.

I knew I'd screw it up. I don't know why I even try.

Not my fault!

I wish everyone would just leave me alone.

Ugh, I'm SO embarrassed!

$¢%@#$%!!!

I'm the worst.

I didn't get it right this time, but that's okay. No big deal.

Whoops. I'm going to try that again—I know I can do it.

Wow, that was really hard. But I'm proud of myself for trying.

Negative Thoughts

Did you notice that there are a lot more "red" thoughts than "green" ones? That's because mistakes often cause us to criticize ourselves. And those negative thoughts can often be a lot stronger than other thoughts.

Our thoughts influence how we feel. So, if you have negative thoughts, you might have negative feelings. Have you ever felt the ACHE of making a mistake? You can feel that ache in different ways. After making a mistake, you may feel:

- embarrassed

- angry at yourself

- like everyone is mad at you

- guilty

- not good enough

- like everyone is staring at you

The ache can also be a real, physical pain that you experience. You may feel:

- sick to your stomach
- red and hot in the face
- sweaty
- shaky
- short of breath

And with different mistakes, you may react differently. If you accidentally call someone the wrong name, you may feel embarrassed for just a second and then move on. If you forget to meet a friend after school, you might feel embarrassed *and* guilty. If you drop your tray in the cafeteria at lunch, you might start sweating from embarrassment. You might want to run and hide. You might even feel bad about yourself, like you can't do anything right.

How do you think you would feel if you made these mistakes?

The score is 1–0, and your team is losing. Only 15 seconds left. Your teammate passes you the puck, and you have a chance to make a goal. You swing your stick back, blast it forward, and . . . whoops! You shank it off to the side. Instead of tying up the game, you lose it for your team.

"Put on your clean black shirt for the concert," your mom says. And then—uh-oh—you realize you didn't put your dirty laundry in the hamper like she told you to. That black shirt is wadded up in the corner of your room, and it is *not* clean. Big mistake.

You didn't study very hard for your social studies test—after all, you always do great in social studies. But when your teacher hands back the graded tests, you didn't do well at all. Several other kids got a perfect score. You know you could have too. You really should have studied.

Your friend invited you to a sleepover at her house, and you said yes. But then a different friend invited you to a movie you've been dying to see. You blow off your first friend to go to the movie with the second friend—and the first friend finds out. Ouch!

Now Playing: The Fair-Weather Friend

Taking Control

No matter how you feel after making a mistake, it's okay to feel like that. Feelings are normal, and we can't control them. But we *can* control what we do after we make a mistake. Taking control and doing something positive can lead to more positive feelings. Sometimes those achy feelings help motivate you to do better next time.

Feel embarrassed that you missed that goal? Maybe you will practice more.

Do you regret not putting your dirty laundry in the hamper when you promised your mom you would? Next time you might remember that yucky feeling and try harder to remember.

Does blowing off a test—and getting a lousy grade—make you mad? Think about that next time you have a test. Maybe you'll study harder to avoid feeling that way again. That ACHE just made you a better student.

And what about getting caught lying to a friend? That can feel really bad. Shameful, even. Apologizing can help your friend *and* you feel better. Promising not to do that again—and *keeping* that promise—can lead to being an even better friend.

The Mistakes People Make After Making a Mistake

It's not always easy to make the right choice about how to react to your mistake. A lot of times, we feel so bad about our mistakes that we add to the problem with how we react. Some people . . .

Deny they made the mistake. "What are you talking about? I didn't leave the freezer door open."

Blame others. *"You made me* forget sunscreen!"

Pretend not to notice. "La la la, dum dee-dum-dum doo."

Give up. "I'll never be any good at this, so why waste my time? If I don't try, I can't fail."

Have you ever done any of these things? Have you done more than one of them? People often try to avoid responsibility for their mistakes in these ways. But as you can probably guess, that's not the healthiest way to react to a mistake. Instead, you can take the ACHE out of mistakes—that's what this book is about (duh).

The first step is understanding what *kinds* of mistakes people make. The next chapter will give you the run-down.

Chapter 2

The Two Main Types of Mistakes

Some mistakes are no big deal. They might be a little frustrating. But you get over them pretty quickly. Other mistakes make you blow your top in anger— KABOOM! Those are the big ones.

Some mistakes affect only you, while others can hurt your friends, parents, teachers, or someone else.

Sometimes your gaffe can make you laugh. Sometimes your blunder is as loud as thunder. And sometimes, just sometimes, your slipups can give you the hiccups. (But really only *sometimes*. Like hardly ever.)

mistake mistake mistake mistake MISTAKE mistake MISTAKE mistake MISTAKE MISTAKE mistake Mistake mistake mistake mistake

There are many, many kinds of mistakes. A good way to start thinking about mistakes is to put them into one of two main categories. Both types can be BIG or small or in between. The categories are:

1. Honest mistakes

2. Intentional mistakes

Honest mistakes include things like forgetting something, accidentally breaking something, or trying to do something and failing (like answering a question in class and getting it wrong).

Intentional mistakes can be things like lying, avoiding responsibility, and doing something else you know is wrong. In all these cases, you know the *right* thing to do. Your mistake is in deciding not to do it.

Honest Mistakes

Have you ever felt like this?

When you mess up in front of others, it can be very embarrassing. It might feel like everyone is laughing at you. Sometimes you just want to crawl away and hide from the world.

It's true, missing a kick in kickball is embarrassing. But don't hide from the world! Missing a kick is an example of an `honest mistake`. Here are a few other examples:

- Dropping something and breaking it

- Spilling your cereal

- Losing something like your keys or phone

- Accidentally farting in front of your friends

- Calling someone by the wrong name

- Missing a dig in volleyball

- Flubbing a line in a play

- Screwing up a skateboard trick

- Messing up the mittens you are knitting

It Was an Accident

An honest mistake has no trickery behind it. There is no selfishness behind it either. Often, you couldn't have even prevented it. It just happens.

Even though the mistake is "honest," most people feel embarrassed to some degree after making a mistake like this. If it's a small mistake, like spilling or dropping something, they usually forget about it soon after. And that's good. These mistakes are small.

Some people have a harder time letting go of a small mistake. They might feel like everyone is laughing at them or judging them. They might even feel like they have a big spotlight on them.

(Don't worry! Chapters 3, 4, and 5 will help you stop feeling like a spotlight is shining on you every time you make a mistake.)

Whoops! (Did You Forget Something?)

One specific kind of honest mistake is common for kids: forgetting.

Everyone forgets to do things sometimes. Unless you're a robot with a computer brain, you have forgotten too. Maybe you forgot to do a chore at home, like take out the garbage.

Or maybe you forgot to text back a friend about homework help.

Maybe you forgot something big, like inviting a friend to your birthday party.

Just like other honest mistakes, forgetting can be anywhere from no big deal to sort of a big deal to a **really** big deal. Using that scale, how would you rate these forgetting mistakes?

No Big Deal? Sort of a Big Deal? Really Big Deal?

I forgot to . . .

- meet my friend at her locker after school and now she's pretty mad
- call my grandma to wish her happy birthday
- feed the dog
- cover my mouth when I coughed
- thank Dad for making dinner
- get ready for soccer practice on time, so I was late
- flush
- zip my zipper
- wear my helmet on my bike
- do my social studies homework
- tell my mom I need a costume for the play— and the play is tomorrow
- stay quiet during silent reading time

Relax! There are no right answers for any of these. It's all about seeing the big picture and recognizing that mistakes come in all different shapes and sizes. And the more you understand your mistakes, the better you can own, fix, and learn from them.

Intentional Mistakes

Sometimes people make mistakes that are not accidents. For example, have you ever said you would do something, but then you didn't do it? Maybe you didn't do it because . . .

Or maybe you didn't do it because . . .

Or maybe it was because . . .

These are all good reasons for not doing something you said you would. But do you know what is **not** a good excuse? Turn the page to find out.

I didn't feel like it.

You may be thinking: "But that's the perfect reason not to do something! Why should I do something if I don't feel like it?"

Here's why: When you don't do something you said you would do, you disappoint the person who was relying on you. You may even cause problems for that person.

Imagine that you've told your little brother that you would take him on a bike ride. He waits for you outside. But you stay in your room playing video games. You've changed your mind. So you blow him off. He probably feels sad and rejected. You have also wasted his time. He could have done something fun rather than just sitting around waiting for you.

Your Behavior Affects Others

Blowing off people is one kind of mistake you can prevent. We call this an *intentional* mistake, because at some point you decided to do what you did—on purpose. That doesn't mean you're a bad person. It means you messed up. And you can choose *not* to mess up next time. Making a more positive choice helps keep your mistake just that—a mistake.

Other kinds of intentional mistakes include lying, cheating, and being mean. Can you guess what these mistakes have in common? One thing is that they are dishonest. The other is written at the top of this page!

That's right: These mistakes affect others.

This is true about intentional mistakes even if you don't *mean* to hurt anyone. For example, when people blow off things, they usually are not trying to be hurtful. They think skipping the task is easier than doing it. They don't want to pull weeds like they're supposed to, so they don't. The math homework is hard, so they avoid it.

Sometimes you don't *mean* to blow off something. You just decide to put it off. And put it off . . . until it's too late. Other times, you may decide right from the start to blow off something. Either way, it's easy to think it's no big deal. After all, it doesn't really affect you.

But it does affect others.

If you don't feed your neighbor's cat when you said you would, the cat goes hungry.

If you don't bring the book your friend needs to write a report, your friend might get a bad grade.

If you don't show up to basketball practice, you might miss an easy layup during a game and cost your team points.

Blowing off things really IS a big deal.

Speak Up

Maybe you really can't do something you said you would. Maybe you are supposed to meet a friend, but you need to do your homework. Or maybe you told your dad you would clean the garage, but you want to take a babysitting job that just came up.

So what do you do? You speak up! Talk to the person who is relying on you and explain the situation. Give a plan for how you will make it up to the person. Here are some examples:

Hey, Omar! I know we are supposed to meet at the skate park today. But I have a killer science test tomorrow that I have to study for. Let's meet after school tomorrow. Okay?

By speaking up ahead of time, you show respect for the person who is relying on you. You show that you know their time and needs are important. You show that you care about the person and that you are a responsible person. And you avoid making the mistake of blowing off something.

If you speak up, it's unlikely the person will get mad at you. (If they do get mad, they probably won't *stay* mad.) Most likely the person will understand. That's typically what happens when you are honest. People around you will trust you, believe you, and want to help make sure things work out for you.

Smell That? (It's Pants on Fire)

Imagine you are a secret agent. It's a hard, dangerous life. You have to fight off angry super-villains and killer razor-tooth piranha bears. You have to chase speeding cars through busy streets and jump off high bridges to *avoid* danger. And, of course, many times you have to lie. After all, you are a *secret* agent, not a run-around-telling-the-truth-all-the-time agent. So if someone wants to know your true identity, you must lie! If someone asks where the key witness is hidden, you must lie! And if someone wants to know who ate the last bagel and thoughtlessly didn't save any for her brother?

Well, you *must* lie, of course.

The TRUTH is, you're probably not a secret agent, but you probably *have* lied. It's another intentional mistake many people make. Sometimes they lie to cover up a problem—especially if they think they might get into trouble. Other times they lie to get out of doing something or to manipulate other people into doing something.

But lying almost never ends well. Lies hurt people around you. And lies hurt you.

Imagine three friends. Maria is jealous that Sophie and Jane are spending a lot of time together. So Maria lies and tells Sophie that Jane said she's getting sick of Sophie. Maria hopes that Sophie and Jane will drift apart.

This lie hurts Sophie. If Sophie gets mad at Jane, then it also hurts Jane. And if the two of them figure out that Maria lied, then Maria will end up getting hurt too. Both Sophie and Jane will be mad at her. And they probably won't include Maria in any of their plans again.

Instead of lying, Maria could tell Sophie and Jane how she feels. They might start to include Maria in more of their activities.

Why Do People Lie?

Lying can lead to hurting others' feelings. It can lead you to feeling guilty and dishonest. And it can be stressful to keep track of who you've lied to and to worry about getting caught. So why do people lie? Usually because it seems easier than telling the truth. Here are a few of the most common reasons.

To avoid disappointing someone. It doesn't feel good when someone is disappointed in you, especially if it's someone you care about, like a parent or good friend. Maybe you accidentally lose a friend's skateboard or run across your dad's garden and wreck his tomatoes. Your friend or your dad is going to be really disappointed. It might seem easier to lie and say it wasn't you.

To avoid being laughed at. If the choice is between lying and being laughed at or made fun of, many would choose lying. Nobody wants to be the butt of jokes. Maybe all your friends have a game on their phones that you don't have, and they make fun of you for not having it. You wish you could get it, too, but you don't have the money right now. You might lie and tell your friends that you already beat that game and now you find it boring.

To avoid punishment. This can be a big one. If you break a rule or do something wrong, you might be in a lot of trouble. You might think: *Maybe I can get out of this! Just deny everything!*

Trying to avoid consequences is a big reason why many people lie. You might even get away with it, at first. But all you're doing is pushing the consequences down the road a little bit. Your bad feelings about lying (or doing whatever you did) are still there. Sooner or later, people are going to find out that you weren't telling the truth. Your bad feelings and their bad feelings will combine into one big, giant, messy, blob of bad feelings—made worse because you lied.

You didn't avoid anything.

To manipulate people. Not all lying is done to avoid consequences. Sometimes people lie to gain something. Maybe they want the teacher to change their grade, so they make up a story about how their mom is really sick and they didn't have a chance to do the homework. Or someone wants the cake you brought in your lunch, so that person tells you he lost his lunch. Maybe you'll feel sorry for him and give him your cake. That's when you've been *manipulated*.

Other times people want to be a part of a certain group of cool kids at school, so they tell lies to make themselves look super-cool or smart or rich. Maybe they lie about where they live so people think their family has more money. Or they lie about things they have or things they have accomplished, like amazing video game scores. Someone might lie about who she's friends with. Or maybe a kid at school is boasting about his score on a test. He wants to show he's better than you and make you feel bad. That's manipulation.

Maybe you can think of times you've told lies like these—so you could get others to do something for you or think higher of you. These lies can be even more harmful to your reputation than other lies. If people learn that you manipulated them, they are likely to be angry. They may never forgive you. They might not ever trust you again. And people might think of you as a liar *and* a manipulator.

Oh, yeah, I used to have that game. I crushed it. I beat it so bad it self-destructed. Smoke was coming up from the tablet, and the lights flickered—you should have seen it. The game's creator called me up, and...

Signs of Lying

Often, when you tell a lie, people know you're lying. They might not tell you that they know—but they know.

How do they know?

Well, your pants go up in *FLAMES*!

Okay, not really. But you do give off other "lying" signals that are almost as obvious as flames. These signals include:

- Your voice may change.

- You may start to breathe more quickly.

- You may pause a lot when speaking.

- You may swallow hard or cough to clear your throat before answering a question.

- You may cover your mouth with your hand.

- Your body may become stiff and tense.

- You may tap your feet nervously.

- You may point at other people to take the focus off yourself.

- You may look away from the person you're lying to.

- You may blink a lot.

People who know you well will definitely recognize these changes. Even people who don't know you very well may recognize that you're behaving uncomfortably. So pretty much everyone will have a good idea that you are lying.

This is Ben. Can you tell when Ben is being honest? Can you tell when he is lying? Turn the page upside-down to check how well you read the signals.

You got it! The Ben on the left couldn't fool you. His lying signals are loud and clear—his body is stiff and tense, he looks nervous, he is tapping his foot, and he is covering his mouth.

Cheating and Being Mean

Cheating and being mean are two other ways to make intentional mistakes. If you cheat on a test, you're being dishonest with your teacher. You're making your teacher think that you prepared for the test and understand the material. What about spreading rumors about someone at school? Rumors are often untrue, and therefore dishonest. But even if the rumor is true, it is still creating a problem for that person. It is mean and unfair.

These kinds of mistakes hurt others. And, just as with lies, you can get caught in these behaviors. Then they hurt you too. Your teacher might figure out that you cheated. Kids at school will think of you as a person who doesn't care about others' feelings.

How will you feel then? Probably not so great.

So what should you do when you make a mistake—honest or intentional? You need to own it, fix it, and learn from it! Keep reading to find out how.

Cheating and being mean is a big category of mistakes. It includes stealing, fighting, bullying, name-calling, and more. Many of these mistakes can be too big to handle on your own. If you've been making bad choices like these, talk to an adult you trust.

Chapter 3

Own your Mistakes

When you make a mistake, there's something you can do to start feeling better about it. Whether it was a big mistake or little one, you can **own it**. In other words: *You messed up, so you need to fess up.* That means you admit to the mistake and take responsibility for it.

Here are some words you can use to own your mistakes. Can you think of others?

For Honest Mistakes

- Oh, shoot, I messed that up.
- That was me.
- My bad!
- Oh, no—I forgot!
- I wish I made that basket, but I missed.
- I can see I didn't study hard enough.

For Intentional Mistakes

- I made a bad choice.
- I should not have done that.
- It was wrong for me to do that.
- I did it.
- I'm the one who shared that mean picture.
- I cheated.

Honest or Intentional?
Don't Confuse the Two

Notice what is *not* on the list of ways to own intentional mistakes: "I forgot." Here's an important rule of mistakes:

No Excuses

When we make mistakes, sometimes we are tempted to try to avoid responsibility. If our mistake affected others, they might be angry with us. We might feel pressure, and we might want to make excuses. See if this story sounds familiar.

THE ADVENTURES OF NO-MISTAKE JAKE

Hi, I'm Jake, and I *never* make a mistake. Ever.

Just today my mom told me to do my laundry. I was totally going to do it. But first I wanted to watch an episode of my favorite streaming show *Dr. What*. It was a good episode. At the end, the doctor's life was in danger, and I couldn't resist watching the next one. I needed to find out what happened! Well, that episode was so good, I got sucked into the next one.

Next thing you know, I had binge-watched five episodes of *Dr. What*. And nobody did the laundry.

When Mom came home later, she saw my pile of dirty clothes still sitting there. If you think she was mad, you're right. "I *told* you to do your laundry!" she fumed. I was in big trouble.

I hate being in trouble.

Then I thought of a way to avoid it. I said, "Sorry, Mom, I thought you said I should do it *tomorrow*." That made it seem like I didn't really do anything wrong. I just misunderstood her.
No mistake here!

Jake thinks he got away with his mistake. He thinks everything is going to be fine. What do you think? His mom knows what she told him: Do the laundry today. She knows that Jake watched TV instead. And now she knows that he lied to her. (Remember those lying signals on page 40? Jake's mom saw a bunch of those signals in Jake.)

Instead of making "no mistake," Jake turned one mistake into two. And he made his mom angrier.

When you're caught making a mistake, it's natural to feel defensive. This may be especially true if you make an intentional mistake like blowing off something. You might feel guilty about what you did, so you want to avoid blame or shift the focus away from yourself. Your first instinct might be to make excuses—or even lie. Don't give in to that temptation. Don't pretend you forgot. Don't pretend you didn't know you were supposed to do it. Don't act like it's someone else's fault, and don't act like it's no big deal.

Instead, remember: If you've blown it, own it.

Why Should You Own Your Mistakes?

Admitting a mistake is not always easy to do. Sometimes it feels embarrassing—or worse, it makes you mad. But in the end, owning your mistake helps you in many ways. Here's why.

Owning your mistake improves your relationships with others. You're honest, so they see that they can trust you. It shows them that you think they are important—too important to lie to.

That doesn't mean people won't be disappointed or even angry about your mistake. It can be hard to face someone you have let down. But that person was probably going to be disappointed or angry anyway. By telling the truth, you let others know that you didn't hurt them on purpose.

Owning your mistakes also improves your relationship with yourself. It doesn't feel good to lie or deny. It can leave you feeling ashamed or angry with yourself. On the other hand, taking responsibility for your mistake can help you feel mature and trustworthy. That's because taking responsibility *is* mature and trustworthy.

It may not feel good to make a mistake. And owning your mistake doesn't make it go away. But it does prevent you—and others—from feeling worse. And you will have grown up a little in the process. Sweet!

Admission Possible

Do you find it hard to admit when you've made a mistake? If that's you, here are two important things you can do to work toward changing.

1. Think about why you have trouble admitting your mistake.

Are you afraid people will get mad at you? Are you afraid they will be disappointed in you? Are you afraid of looking less than perfect?

These are all reasonable fears. No one wants people mad at them. Nobody wants to disappoint others. And who wants to look like some kind of mistake-making bumbler? Nobody.

Try to remember that mistakes are natural. Just like everyone else, you will definitely forget to do things—even really important things. You will accidentally hurt someone's feelings. You will try hard to do something and mess it up. Admitting your mistakes doesn't make you a worse person. It means you have courage and honesty.

Even intentional mistakes are part of life. Everyone makes bad decisions sometimes. Admitting your mistake means you are ready to fix it. It means you are ready to make a better choice next time.

2. Remember that with many mistakes, you are probably letting someone else down.

If your mistake affects other people, they may get mad at you. Here are other ways people might feel when you forget to do what you said you would do, blow them off, or screw up something that affects them:

Frustrated

Irritated

Annoyed

Sad

Betrayed

Disappointed

If you are caught forgetting, messing up, or being hurtful, don't act like it's nothing. That just makes the other person even more upset, like the person's feelings don't matter to you.

Got Away with It?

Sometimes you might get away with an intentional mistake. The person you lied to believes you. Or you blew off a chore or homework and nobody said a word. What do you think happens then? Do you feel like a huge success? Do you think you get praise for being a super blower-offer? Are you the awesomest, hot-shottest, big-time lyingest liar?

You probably know that's not what happens. Not even close.

Instead, people who "get away" with being dishonest often end up in the . . .

WORRY PIT!

Once in the worry pit, people often feel bad about themselves. They might even feel ashamed. They worry that their dishonesty will be discovered. They fear that everyone will get mad at them if their intentional mistake is revealed. They might have a hard time sleeping. Maybe they suffer from stomachaches. Maybe they even feel like a fake.

Who wants to feel like that? Nobody.

So avoid the worry pit. Try not to lie or be dishonest—even if you think you can get away with it. Sometimes choosing to make an intentional mistake might feel like the easy way out of a problem. But in the end, it only makes things worse. The honest and right way to deal with a problem may be harder, but you'll feel muuuuch better for it.

Chapter 4
Fix Your Mistakes

Owning your mistake is important. But it's only the first part of successfully handling a mistake. The second part is to **fix it**. This means apologizing to anyone who may have been affected by your mistake. And it means trying to make things better.

APOLOGIZING + MAKING THINGS BETTER = FIXING YOUR MISTAKE

Both parts of the equation are important. Apologizing *and* making up for your mistake go together like a bike goes with wheels. The apology is the bike. It's a great machine, right? It can get you far in life. But it can't take you anywhere without the wheels.

All About Apologizing

If your mistake affected someone else, the first step is to apologize. Some people are champs at saying, "I'm sorry. I'll fix it." Other people have trouble admitting even the tiniest of mistakes. Which one are you? Answer these questions to find out. (And be honest!)

1. You forgot to clean the bathroom. Now your dad wants to know what happened. What do you say?

   A: Whoops! I forgot. Sorry, I'll do it now.

   B: Why do I always have to clean the bathroom?

2. Your friend lent you a book, and you lost it. Your friend asks about the book. What do you say?

   A: I'm so sorry, I lost it. I will buy you a new one.

   B: You already read it, so what's the big deal?

3. You got a text that made fun of a girl in your class, and you forwarded it to others. The girl finds out and gets mad at you. What do you say?

   A: I'm really sorry! It must have been really hurtful to you. I should have deleted it instead of passing it along.

   B: Don't blame me, I didn't start it.

Did you answer all A's? Congrats! You are a Saying Sorry Superstar. Keep reading this chapter to reinforce your good habits and learn mistake-fixing strategies.

For everyone else, congrats to you too! Why congrats? Because you are reading this book. You know you need help with making up for mistakes. You are on the right path to becoming a champ at saying, "I'm sorry. I'll fix it." So keep reading.

The Ingredients of a Sincere Apology

Check out these examples of apologies for mistakes that affect others. Can you tell what they have in common?

I'M so sorry!

I wasn't honest before.

The truth is _____.

Can you forgive me?

It was really mean when I said _____ to you. I shouldn't have done that.

I'M really sorry.

I will never be mean to you again.

When I did _____, I made a big mistake.

I did it because _____. I'M truly sorry.

How can I make it up to you?

> I'm very sorry I _____.
>
> I feel terrible.
>
> I never should have done that.
>
> What can I do to make it better?

Did you notice what all of these apologies have in common? They all:

- Own the mistake. Not a single one includes an excuse.

- Try to fix the situation. Each one includes an apology and a way of making it up to the person.

It's not always easy to know how to make up for a mistake. Often, it's enough to promise not to do whatever you did to the person anymore. Sometimes you might have to tell the truth to other people who were affected. If you're not sure what to do, it is always a good idea to simply ask: "How can I make it up to you?" The other person might say it's all good—your apology was enough. But what if they say it's *not* good enough? You can read more about fixing mistakes later in this chapter.

HOW TO BE A **WISE WORD CHOOSER**

When it's time to apologize, make sure you choose the right words for the right audience. You don't want to talk to your teacher or parent like you would talk to a friend.

A friend might find this apology to be perfectly fine. But talking to your teacher like this won't win you any points. Teachers deserve your respect. And this way of talking does not show it. Because of that, it probably won't get you want you want—an extension on your homework.

Instead, you want to talk to your teacher like, well, you would talk to a teacher. You need to be polite and respectful.

Did you hear the difference? This apology shows manners and respect for the teacher's authority. It shows that you know the decision about whether you can turn in your homework late is up to your teacher.

Saying sorry—and choosing your words wisely—sounds pretty simple, right? Still, it can be hard to know exactly what to say, especially if you're not used to admitting your mistakes or apologizing. Here are some great phrases you can use:

I'M so sorry. That was wrong of Me. I feel really bad. How can I Make it up to you?

I can't believe I Messed that up! Sorry! I'll do it again right now.

I completely forgot about that. I apologize. What can I do to Make the situation better?

If you are not used to apologizing, you might want to practice. You can practice in a mirror. You can practice with a friend. Saying the words out loud will make you more comfortable with them. Then, when you make a mistake, you'll know exactly what to say.

How to Be a Top-Notch Fixer

Are you comfortable with saying sorry but unsure of how to *fix* your mistakes? If your mistake affected someone else, you have to fix it whether it was an intentional mistake (like a lie) or an honest one (like forgetting). Here are some common mistakes—and what to do about them.

Forgot your homework? See if you can turn it in late. You might get partial credit, and your teacher will be impressed that you care enough to make it right.

Blew off a chore? Do the chore now. After all, the vacuuming—or dishes or kitty litter box cleaning or another job—still needs to be done. Better late than never.

Trampled your neighbor's garden while playing tag? Offer to buy new plants and plant them. If you can't afford it, offer to do chores for the neighbor.

Said something mean about another person? Say something nice. Stick up for that person when others are mean. Make a promise that you will not do that again. That shows you care about this person's feelings.

Forgot your grandfather's birthday? Make him a nice card—and maybe call him too!

Sometimes it's hard to know how to fix a mistake. When you're unsure, there's one thing that always works: Ask!

- I messed up. I should have been there. I'm really sorry. **How can I make it up to you?**

- I didn't mean to hurt your feelings. You have every right to be mad at me. **Is there anything I can do to make things better between us?**

- You're right—I blew it off. I'm sorry. You are important to me. **What can I do to make it right?**

Just like apologizing, it can be helpful to practice saying these phrases by yourself. That way, when it comes time to use them, you'll be more comfortable.

Chapter 5

Learn from your Mistakes

You made a mistake. But you owned it. And you fixed it. For that, you can feel good about yourself. But there's something else you can do to really de-ACHE your mistake. You can do this whether your mistake was honest or intentional. You can do it if your mistake affected someone else or only affected you.

You can almost always learn something from your mistake.

Learning from mistakes is how we get better at things. It's how we grow as people and become smarter, more mature, and better prepared for future challenges. This applies to big, embarrassing, super-terrible mistakes as well as teeny-tiny ones.

I'm going to get this song right eventually.

Here are some examples of how you can learn from honest mistakes:

Missed the ball in kickball? Maybe you were trying to kick too hard, and you need to focus on contact. Maybe you were distracted. Maybe you just need more practice. That's a great way to learn.

Made mittens with multiple thumbs? Just working on the mittens makes you better at knitting—you're learning to do better. If you can figure out why you messed up, you learn even more.

Got a low grade on your book report? Figure out if you misunderstood the directions. Ask your teacher to help you understand how you could have done better. Maybe you tried to write it at the last second instead of giving yourself more time. Maybe you simply need more practice at writing. Well, guess what? That's what you got when you wrote the report! You're learning to write better. And next time you'll be a little better at it.

These kinds of honest mistakes have something in common: Before you can make them, you have to *try* something. You tried kickball and missed. You tried knitting and screwed up. For all these mistakes, part of learning is built into the mistake. Just trying that activity and screwing up makes you better at it. Still, these mistakes might be extra painful because of that. It might feel like you signed up for your own mess up! After all, if you hadn't decided to knit those mittens, you never would have made such a "thumb" mistake.

To avoid that frustration, some people might try to pretend that they didn't make a mistake—or that they did it on purpose. Check out this story.

THE ADVENTURES OF NO-MISTAKE JAKE

Remember me? I'm No-Mistake Jake. And when I say "no mistake," I mean it. I never make mistakes.

For example, yesterday I was playing chess with my good friend Izzie. I taught her how to play a few weeks ago, and she's gotten really good! Not as good as me, of course. So yesterday, when she captured my queen, it might have *looked* like I made a bad move. It might have *looked* like she was about to beat me, fair and square. But that's

not true! The truth is, I purposely let her take my queen. Just to prove it, I made another really bad move after that. "Here, take my stupid rook," I said. I didn't care— it wasn't a real game anyway. I was just helping her learn. I mean, she couldn't beat me if I were really trying. No way, no how. Sorry, Izzie. I'm still the best.

Jake is telling himself—and Izzie and anyone else who will listen—that he did not mess up. He *let* his friend win. But really, he's just covering up for his mistake. It's too hard for him to admit that he lost. Do you know anyone who has done that?

Have you ever done that?

The truth is, Jake made a mistake in his game, and he lost. And he should feel great about that! Why? Any time you play a game against others . . .

or challenge yourself to try something new . . .

or take a chance on something that's hard . . .

or pursue an interest . . .

or do anything else that involves possible success and failure, you are growing as a person. And you should feel *good*—not bad!

Maybe you've never baked a cake before, and you decide to give it a try. Pat yourself on the back for expanding your horizons. Give a big, "Yay, me!" for working to make yourself more rounded, more experienced, more interesting . . . and more interest*ed*. Because having interests is what makes life great.

It's not just about trying something new. Even if you have been knitting for a year, you might still make mistakes. Or if you've competed in dozens of races, you still might post a bad time. Or you might forget the lyrics to a song you've sung tons of times. Or make a bad move in a game you've played a lot. You are still trying to get better, right? You're still challenging yourself, still trying to accomplish things, and still trying to have fun.

You, just like anyone who tries things—even famous people—are guaranteed to make mistakes. And when you do, **you are learning**.

Michael Jordan is a basketball legend. He has six—SIX—NBA championship rings. He was named most valuable player 14 times. Here's what he has to say about his success:

"I've missed more than 9,000 shots in my career. I've lost almost 300 games. Twenty-six times, I've been trusted to take the game-winning shot and missed. I've failed over and over and over again in my life. And that is why I succeed."

Here's the most important thing to remember about these kinds of mistakes:

They are proof of trying.

They mean you care.

They mean you want to succeed at something.

And they increase the chance that you *will* succeed.

Oh, that was RUFF!

Learn from Forgetting

Not all mistakes are proof of trying. If you forgot to text your friend back . . . well, you just forgot. But you can still learn from your forgetting mistakes. For example, when you forget something and let down someone, you can learn a lot about how your behavior affects others. You can learn why it's important to keep your word. And that might lead you to do a better job of remembering in the future. Most importantly, you can learn *how* to do better next time.

Why is that important? Because if you keep forgetting things, even little things, it can become a big problem. Friends, family, teachers, and other adults might lose their patience with you. They might start to think you are irresponsible. They may even stop trusting you.

Forgetting can cause other problems too. You can miss out on important things like music practice and going to the movies with friends. Your grades might suffer if you keep forgetting things like homework and tests. You might lose friends or get in trouble with your parents if you let them down too many times. You might repeat mistakes you could have avoided.

Here are some tips to help you forget about forgetting and start remembering:

`Keep a calendar.` Mark homework due dates and plans with your friends on your calendar. Mark other important events on your calendar too. Check your calendar every morning to see what you are supposed to do that day. Look ahead a few days, too, so you can prepare for what's coming. If your calendar is on your phone or tablet, set alarms to help remind you when you need to do certain things.

Make lists. Do you need to get specific supplies for an art project? Do you need to find certain books at the library? Do you have another list of things you need to remember? Write your list in a notebook. Or enter it into your phone or tablet.

Leave notes for yourself. Maybe your mom says, "Please meet your little brother at the bus stop after school today—about 20 minutes after you get home." You say, "Sure!" and then you forget all about it. Instead, say, "Sure!" and then leave a big note for yourself, maybe on the back of your desk chair or on the refrigerator handle. Leave it where you won't miss seeing it when you get home that day.

Get into a routine. Routines help you remember things. If your chore is to empty the dishwasher, empty it as soon as you get home from school every day. Soon, you will automatically walk into the kitchen after getting home. You won't even have to remind yourself.

You can come up with your own ways of remembering. The important thing isn't *how* you remember, but *that* you remember! The more you remember to do the things that you said you would do, the less you will have to say, "Whoops, I forgot! I'm sorry!"

Learn from Blowing Off Things

What about blowing off things? That is an intentional mistake that you can stop making. If you don't, you will send a big, loud message to everyone around you that you do not care about their time or needs. People will start to think that you are irresponsible. They will likely form other negative opinions about you. Here are a few ways people might react if you keep blowing off things.

Like forgetting things, blowing off things is a mistake that can teach you a lot. Think about how your behavior affects others. Who did you let down? Who had to do the work you skipped? How else were others affected? How did they feel? Most importantly, how can you make sure it doesn't happen again?

If blowing off things is a mistake you often make, you can break the habit. How? Start thinking in a new way.

If you think this . . .	Think this instead . . .
It's not a big deal if I don't do it.	It's a big deal to the person who asked me, so I should do it.
She shouldn't have asked me in the first place.	I should have said "no." But since I said "yes," I need to do it.
I can just say that I forgot.	They will know I'm lying.
I'd rather do something else. Having to do this task is so annoying.	Having someone mad at me will be much worse.
I've gotten away with it before.	I'll feel better about myself if I live up to my word.

Thinking about how your behavior affects other people (and yourself) will help you change your behavior.

Learn from Lying

If you told a lie—and you apologized and tried to fix it—you probably learned a lot. You saw how others were hurt, frustrated, or inconvenienced. Think about how it felt to be dishonest. Remember that feeling the next time you are tempted to tell a lie. This is what you have learned: It doesn't feel good.

Some people lie a lot. They do it even if they regret lying. And even though they know that it only causes them stress, they can't stop themselves. For them, stopping can be even harder. But they can learn the same lessons about feelings and consequences.

Whether you lie often or hardly ever, you can learn to do better at telling the truth. Here are some tips to help you:

Figure out why you lie. Do you lie to avoid disappointing people? Maybe you need to learn how to be okay with people being unhappy with you every so often. Do you lie to avoid **ridicule**? You may need to work on building your self-esteem. Talk with a parent or other adult, or an older sibling, about overcoming whatever it is you're afraid of. It's also a good idea to talk to someone if you're lying to manipulate others. Ask someone you trust for help with being more honest. Your school guidance counselor might be a good person to start with. He or she can help you figure out how serious your problem is—and, if needed, connect you with other people who can help you.

Think about how you feel after you lie. Do you end up in that worry pit? Do you feel guilty? Do you feel lower than low when you are caught in a lie? These are all good reasons to stop lying. Then you can feel good about yourself instead.

Play out in your mind how things could have gone. Imagine that you had told the truth. Imagine how people would have reacted. Imagine how you would have felt. You probably will discover that you felt better than when you lied.

Practice telling the truth. Do you have a tough moment coming up where you might be inclined to lie? Practice what you will say. Think of all the ways people may respond. Practice reacting to them with the truth.

Switching from lying to telling the truth might feel uncomfortable at first. You might feel unprotected, as if everyone can see right through you or easily hurt you. But soon, you will find strength in the truth. And the more you stop the lies, the stronger you will get.

After you've stopped lying, you'll probably feel a lot better about yourself. But if you have been lying for a long time, some people might not believe the new you. They might think you're lying even when you're telling the truth. This might be frustrating, but it's understandable. **Building trust takes time.** You'll have to show for a long time that you are honest before people will see you that way.

Learn from Other Intentional Mistakes

In some ways, intentional mistakes like cheating, bullying, or purposely hurting another person are just like lying. To learn from these other intentional mistakes, think about how your behavior affected others. Think about why you did what you did. Then work hard to stop doing these things.

Intentional mistakes are usually bigger than other mistakes. They can be more hurtful to others and yourself. They might lead to even bigger mistakes in the future. And they can be harder to stop, especially if you do them often. You may need an adult to help you learn from and stop these behaviors. Think of an adult you trust, like a parent, a teacher, a counselor, or an older sibling. Tell this person what you've been doing and that you want to stop.

It will probably feel scary to admit this to someone, especially a grown-up. Sometimes the biggest thing you can learn from a mistake is courage—the courage to change. You can do it!

Chapter 6

Nobody's Perfect
(And you're Not Nobody)

You probably like to do well at the things you try. Most people do. Who wouldn't prefer to get an A on a math test instead of a B or C? Or hit a home run instead of strike out? Or what if you have to give a presentation in class? You'd probably rather do a great job and look smart in front of everyone than mess up.

It's great to work hard to try to be successful. It's even great to try to be excellent. Pushing yourself to improve is very healthy. That's how people grow. But there is a big difference between trying to do well and feeling like a failure if you make a mistake.

Consider two friends, Isra and Jana. They both are strong students and work hard in school. One day they get their social studies tests back from their teacher. They each lost a point on one question, but they both got an A. Isra looks at her test and feels great about her grade. She reads her teacher's comment about why she lost that point so she understands how to do better next time. By the next day, she has pretty much forgotten about the test.

But Jana is really frustrated, and a bad feeling nags at her for the rest of the week. She can't stop thinking about the point she lost. She calls herself names like *stupid* and *lazy.* She worries that the other students think she's dumb. She doesn't even tell her parents about the test because she doesn't want them to know that she was less than perfect.

Jana did a great job. But she is a perfectionist. She doesn't feel proud of her accomplishment because of the one mistake she made.

What Is Perfectionism?

Perfectionism is wanting to be perfect at the things you do. But more than that, it's a *fear* of being less than perfect. Fear is the main difference between someone who wants to be perfect and someone who just really wants to be good at things. People who want to be good at things can be less than perfect and still feel okay. They might be disappointed in their grade or performance, but they don't feel crushed by it. People who are perfectionists are afraid that making mistakes or coming in second place means something is wrong with them.

But everyone makes mistakes. People who want to be perfect end up feeling anxious or worried *a lot* of the time. That fear weighs on them in just about everything they do. They think that if they make a mistake, others will see them as failures. They think they have to be the best at everything they do. They think that they are awesome when they do everything right but terrible when they make mistakes. They criticize themselves for their mistakes, and they take others' criticisms very personally.

Perfectionists even think people might stop being their friend if they make a mistake. Or their parents may not love them if they're not perfect. So they make the biggest mistake of all—they do everything they can to avoid making any mistake.

Why It's Hard to Be Perfectionistic

Being someone who wants to be perfect is hard. The pressure of always having to win and never being able to accept a mistake can be suffocating. It feels awful to be so hard on yourself when you mess up or lose. Here are some of the ways that perfectionism can affect your life.

Not Enjoying Things

People who seek perfection tend to focus on the end result and not on the process of getting there. So, if you are working on a science project with a friend, you don't enjoy brainstorming ideas. You only want to identify the perfect idea for your science project. You don't have fun exploring the different ways you could build your science project. And you definitely don't have a good time building it. You hardly find it interesting. Instead you feel agitated and pressured. You want the project to be finished so you can get an A on it.

People who need to be perfect may spend hours, even days, working on a project like that. Often, they don't enjoy a single moment of that time. They're not "in the moment" because they're worried about the results.

Perfectionism steals your ability to have fun.

Missing Out on Things

No one wants to be a failure—especially not someone who wants to be perfect. So perfectionists tend to avoid challenging themselves or trying things they might fail at. Maybe you really want to play the lead role in the school play. But you can't bear the idea of trying out for it and not getting the part. You try out for a smaller part instead.

You get the small part, and you're happy—sort of. You can't help wondering whether you should have tried out for the lead. But tryouts are over, and you can't turn back time. You may always wonder whether you could have been fantastic in the lead role.

Perfectionism cheats you out of the chance to discover something about yourself.

Aiming Low

Some people who seek perfection are so afraid of not being perfect that they aim really, *really* low—as in, they don't try to achieve anything. They don't try to make a homemade birthday card for their friend. That way, they don't have to discover that they might not be a great artist. Or they blow off reading their language arts assignment and they don't study for the social studies test. That way, if they get a bad grade, they can tell themselves that it doesn't reflect their real skills. After all, they didn't even try! They don't participate in sports, so they can never look clumsy on the field. They don't even let their grandpa teach them how to play gin rummy because they don't want to make any mistakes in front of him. Instead, they do just the bare minimum to get by. If they don't try anything new or different, then they can't fail.

The trouble with that is, trying your best is how you get better at things. Challenging yourself is good for you. And trying new things is fun!

Perfectionism robs you of opportunities to learn new skills and have new achievements—and feel great about yourself.

THE ADVENTURES OF NO-MISTAKE JAKE

This week in class, I got really excited because we started talking about the International Space Station—the ISS. I love everything about outer space and space exploration. I read that the latest payload going up to the ISS had books on it that the astronauts would read on video for kids to watch. Super cool!

But when Mr. Jenkins asked about it in class, I kind of froze. For some reason, I was afraid to speak up. Sure, I read a lot about the ISS. And sure, I'm pretty much the smartest guy you've ever met . . . but what if I said something wrong? Or what if I asked a question and everyone else already knew the answer?

I mean it probably wouldn't happen. After all, I'm super smart.

But what if it did?

Then people might think I don't know everything. They might think I'm . . . less than brilliant. And I didn't want anyone to think that. So I decided not to take a chance on saying something dumb. Instead, I didn't say anything at all.

I just sat there and listened to Mr. Jenkins and the other students, but it was boring. They didn't talk about anything I didn't already know. In the end, the space discussion was a big letdown.

Jake worries that people will think less of him if he isn't perfect. He knows a lot about the ISS, but he can't stand the thought that someone else might not think so. He thinks he's playing it safe by staying quiet. But in the end, he missed out on something he would have enjoyed.

Now *that* is a true mistake.

Obsessing Over Things

People who seek perfection tend to overthink every little detail. Imagine you have to make a model of the solar system. You spend hours researching the gases of Mars's atmosphere so that you can figure out the exact shade of red to paint your Mars ball—when you *could* pick a good shade of red paint just by spending a few minutes researching pictures of Mars online. If you spend that much time on every planet, you'll never finish your project in time.

This worrying about details is not limited to schoolwork. People who want to be perfect sometimes have to have their things a certain way. They might remake their bed several times every morning so that it is just right—even though nobody else would be able to tell the difference between the first attempt and the final one. They might keep the books on their shelf in a very particular order—and get mad if anyone messes up that order. Then they have to reorganize the book shelf to get it exactly right again.

Perfectionism wastes a lot of your time.

Feeling Like a Failure

Perfectionists have really high standards. Their standards may even be impossible to reach. Imagine you decide that you're going to get an A on every project, every paper, every quiz, and every test all year long. Then you get a B on a quiz. You haven't lived up to your standards, so you feel like a failure. You get mad at yourself. You feel like you can't do anything right. Your confidence drops. You think people don't like you because you are such a big loser. And you start not liking yourself.

Criticizing Yourself

One of the hardest things for perfectionists is how they treat themselves. They trash themselves with their self-talk. Self-talk is how you talk to yourself in your mind. Have you ever said anything like the phrases below to yourself?

You wouldn't call your friend an idiot. And you wouldn't tell your mom or sister that she isn't good enough. Nobody deserves to hear such mean comments. So why would anyone say things like this to themselves? It's hard for perfectionists to remember that making mistakes is part of being human.

Are You Someone Who Seeks Perfection?

Take this quiz to find out.

1. A week ago, you handed in your homework a day late. How do you feel about it today?

   A: I'm still really embarrassed about it.

   B: I haven't really thought about it since.

2. Your class is organizing a walk-a-thon to raise money for the school library. How is the experience going?

   A: I'm frustrated! Everyone talks about everything way too much without ever making a decision.

   B: I'm having a great time! Talking through all the decisions is really fun.

3. You were on the debate team last year. You lost your last debate. Will you join the team again this year?

   A: No, I don't want to look like a fool again for losing.

   B: For sure! I'm excited to show that I can do better this year.

4. How much time did you spend on a model of the Great Pyramid for your social studies unit?

   A: Hours every day for two weeks. I had to make sure it was scaled perfectly to the real pyramid.

   B: About six hours total. My model looks pretty much like a smaller version of the real thing.

5. Think about your day so far. How many times have you criticized yourself for not being perfect?

   A: Several times. I really hate when I don't do something the right way.

   B: Zero times. I can deal with it when I make a mistake.

Did you answer all or mostly A's? You might be someone who wants perfection. You might want to talk to your parents or your school guidance counselor to see if you really have an issue with perfectionism. The next few pages give some great tips for letting go of perfectionism. The list of resources at the end of this book might also be helpful for easing up on yourself and learning to be okay with mistakes.

Did you answer all or mostly B's? You probably are not perfectionistic. But keep reading on. The next few pages give good information about ways to feel good about yourself while trying to aim for greatness.

Letting Go of Perfectionism

It's important to remember that there's a difference between trying to do well and being a perfectionist. It's always okay—in fact it's great—to shoot for excellence. But if you struggle with perfectionism, it might help to remember that mistakes, even major failures, can help you in life.

That's right: Mistakes can `help` you.

Mistakes Are Exercise for Your Brain

When you make a mistake and then try again, your brain actually gets stronger. Your brain gets stronger if you get the wrong answer on a math question and try again. It gets stronger if you try to fix your bike chain and mess up and then try again. Your brain gets stronger any time you make a mistake and try again.

Here's how it works. When you make a mistake and try again, the neurons in your brain fire up. They send signals to each other. The connections between the neurons get stronger. The next time you are in a similar situation, your brain will act faster to figure out how to tackle that situation. With every mistake, your brain gets better at putting you in position to handle future challenges.

But this doesn't mean you should make mistakes or mess things up on purpose. Improvements happen when you *try* to do well—and then try again. So give yourself a break when you naturally make mistakes going after goals and challenging yourself. What you should really fear is *never* making a mistake. Because then your brain never gets the "mistake" chance to become stronger.

Some Tools to Try

Here are a few tools—activities and experiments—you can use to help you get over your perfectionism.

List what's good about you. You are good at lots of things, and you have lots of good qualities. Write them down. Perfectionists are often hard workers. If that's you, add it to your list. If you have high standards, that's a good quality too. Put it on your list. If you're a good friend, if you're good at checkers, if you know a lot about history or dinosaurs or soccer . . . put it on your list. Making a list of your good

qualities—caring, responsible, honest, cooperative— can help you start thinking about yourself in a better light. You *are* good enough, even if you're not perfect!

Get started quickly. Some people who seek perfection put off doing things like schoolwork or projects because they're afraid of messing up. If fear of mistakes makes you procrastinate, try jumping into a task or your homework. Start right away without thinking too much about it—start before you're really ready. Tell yourself you can fix things later, but for now just start.

Put someone else in your shoes. When you make a mistake or don't do something as well as you'd like, imagine that someone else made that mistake instead. Maybe you got a B on your science homework, and you're really upset about it. You even call yourself a loser. Stop and imagine that your best friend got the B. Would you think of your best friend as a loser? Probably not. You would probably not be nearly as hard on your friend as you are on yourself. In fact, you'd probably think your friend did a pretty good job. Try to remember to treat yourself the same way.

Try looking on the bright side. On page 99, you learned about self-talk. That's how you talk to yourself in your head. When you make a mistake, you can change your self-talk to treat yourself a little better. Look at this table for examples.

If you think . . .	Try thinking . . .
I can't believe I made such a terrible pass in soccer!	My pass was off, but passing has always been hard for me. I am getting better.
I'm not going to join the chess club after school. I'll just lose all the time.	It's true I might lose a lot in chess club. But I will get better by playing against strong opponents.
Everyone thought I was stupid when I said the wrong answer in class.	I said the wrong answer, but now I understand how to do that math problem better. I'll nail it on the test.
I got another C in science. I'm such an idiot!	Science is a hard subject for me. But I am proud that I keep trying. I know I'll get better.

Ask for help. It can be really helpful to talk to an adult you trust about your fear of making mistakes. Your parent, teacher, aunt or uncle, or other grown-up can help put mistakes in perspective. What should you talk about? Ask the adult what he or she thinks is good about you, and add it to your list. Tell him or her about your fears and perfectionism. Ask if the adult has ever felt that way. If so, how did he or she deal with it? Getting these fears into the open can be a big help.

GREAT MISTAKES

Letting go of your need to be perfect can be difficult—even when you know that mistakes can help you improve and grow. It might help you to read about some really great mistakes—mistakes that led to positive changes and important progress.

- One day in 1853, a chef in a restaurant got a complaint from a customer: His fried potatoes were too thick and soft. The chef, who had a short temper, got frustrated. So he sliced the potatoes as thin as he possibly could, then fried them in oil until they were hard and crunchy. *Happy now?* he must have thought. To his surprise, though, the customer *was* happy—he loved them. The thinly fried potatoes were added to the menu and eventually became one of the most well-loved snacks of all time: the potato chip. Thanks, grumpy chef!

- A chemist was trying to make a really tough type of rubber to use on airplanes. Her assistant dropped a bottle of one solution she had mixed for the rubber, and it splashed onto the chemist's white sneakers. The solution didn't damage or change the color of the sneakers, so she kept wearing them. Later, she noticed that the part that had been splashed never got dirty. She realized that she had invented a fabric protector! Today, her solution is used on furniture and carpets to protect them from stains.

- One sloppy scientist left his petri dishes unwashed. He later found that many of them had grown bacteria colonies. In one dish, however, he saw that a patch of mold had prevented the bacteria from growing. The mold was penicillin, and its ability to kill deadly bacteria has saved countless lives since then.

- An 11-year-old boy left his glass of soda outside overnight in the winter with a stirring stick in it. Silly mistake, right? When he found his drink the next morning, it was frozen solid with the stick poking out the top. He grabbed the stick and pulled the drink out of the glass. Years later he patented his invention as "Popsicles."

Not every mistake is going to lead to the invention of a tasty new treat or a life-saving medicine. In fact, most won't. But all these people owned their mistakes and learned from them. When you do that, things usually work out for the better.

Go for It!

In chapter 5, you learned that mistakes are proof of trying. They show that you have the courage to challenge yourself. People who audition for a play are brave. People who raise their hands to answer in class are risking that they might be wrong in front of everyone. People who go for it look like they fear nothing.

So if perfectionism leads you to avoid challenges so you don't risk looking like a failure, try embracing challenges instead. Do you want that lead role? Go for it! Do you think you know the answer to the math problem? Raise your hand!

You might find it scary at first to go for things when you are used to avoiding them. But the more you go for it, the braver you will start to feel. Your self-esteem will grow too. You'll start to feel more and more like you can handle challenges and get past obstacles. You won't just be giving off the *appearance* that you are courageous, you will actually *become* a courageous person.

Chapter 7

Don't Forget to Forgive

Some kids have a hard time letting go of a mistake. Even after they have owned, fixed, and learned from their mistake, they still beat themselves up about it. If that's you, you can learn to forgive yourself. Here are a few things you can do to change how you feel about mistakes—and about yourself.

Be Kind to Yourself

When you mess up, treat yourself with kindness. To see how to do this, talk to yourself the way you would talk to a friend. You would never say to a friend, "I can't believe you gave the wrong answer in math class. You're such a dummy." So don't say it to yourself.

Give Yourself a Mental Break

Another way to start feeling better about mistakes is to give yourself a mental break. If, after making a mistake, you start to criticize yourself, follow these steps:

1. Close your eyes.

2. Slow down your breathing.

3. Relax your muscles.

4. Think about absolutely nothing for two or three minutes.

5. Open your eyes.

Taking a mental break stops the rush of negative thoughts from filling your mind. It clears your mind, so your mind has room for kind thoughts. Taking a mental break can also lower your blood pressure. It can calm you down. When you are calm, you are less likely to throw angry words at yourself. You are more likely to see your mistake as just that—a mistake. And you are more likely to have the mental space to learn from your mistake.

Don't Worry About the Spotlight

If you have trouble letting go of even the smallest of mistakes, here's a really BIG truth to think about: Most people don't pay much attention to other people's mistakes. Why? Because most people are too busy thinking about *themselves* to be thinking about *you*.

Sure, if you whiff in kickball, people might laugh at first. You may feel a huge spotlight is shining on you. But then the game moves on. The next ball is rolled, and the next play is made. Everyone is thinking about their own game, not yours. And that spotlight? It's long gone.

Think about it. What is the last mistake you can remember your best friend making? What about your mom or dad? What about one of your teachers? It's guaranteed that they have all made mistakes over the past few weeks, yet you probably can't remember any of them.

And when it comes to your small mistakes, in a week or two, nobody will remember yours either.

Forgive Others

Everybody makes mistakes. And sometimes, the mistakes other people make will affect you. You might feel hurt or frustrated. What should you do when that happens? Throw a fit! Yell. Scream. Turn a HUGE spotlight on the person. Tell them they are terrible. Tell them . . .

All right. You know that's the exact OPPOSITE of what you should do. You know the right thing to do— the fair, *kind* thing. Calmly tell the person how the mistake has affected you. Give them a chance to fix the mistake. And forgive the person, just like you would want that person to forgive you.

A Note for Parents and Teachers

All parents want their children to succeed and be the best that they can be. Teachers want the same thing for their students. So it can be painful to see a child miss a free throw during a game, freeze up when giving a speech in class, or make another kind of mistake. And if kids have a difficult time dealing with mistakes, watching them become embarrassed or self-critical over even the smallest of mistakes can be even more painful.

For many of us, our instinct is to rush in and fix the situation. But it's important to remember that we all make mistakes. And learning how to deal with mistakes is part of growing up and becoming a successful adult. Instead of fixing mistakes for our kids, the best course of action is to guide them through owning the mistake, fixing it themselves, and learning from it.

Here are some tips for how to do that:

Keep your anger in check. Expressing anger at kids over a mistake will likely make them feel a deeper embarrassment or even shame about the mistake. Those feelings could keep them from owning their mistake and learning from it—and that would be the real mistake.

Explain that it's okay to make a mistake. Point out that everyone makes mistakes, and no one should feel like a failure, strange, or unlikable for making a mistake.

Validate feelings. Recognize that even though everyone makes mistakes, it can still be embarrassing when you're the one who has made one. It can even be frustrating. Explain that these feelings are normal. How you handle the feelings is what is important.

Encourage ownership of the mistake. Help your child or student say, "Yep, that was me. I did it." You can do this by creating a safe environment for kids to own their mistakes, free from judgment. Teach everyone in the class or family to think of mistakes as learning opportunities, so when someone does make a mistake, peers are encouraging and supportive. When consequences are necessary, say, for an intentional mistake, choose consequences that are appropriate for the mistake and not overly harsh.

Resist the urge to rescue—but help as needed. Though protecting kids is a natural inclination, it's important to stand back and let kids fix their own mistakes. Provide support and encouragement when needed. Big mistakes can feel overwhelming, and kids may need an adult perspective and guidance. Guiding is not the same as rescuing. Let kids take the lead, and be available. Provide examples of ways they can fix the situation. But let them implement the guidance themselves.

Use mistakes as teachable moments. Help children see what they can learn from the mistake. Learning from a mistake is one of the best ways to avoid repeating it.

Be a constant in their lives. Make sure your children know you love them or that your students know you respect them. Sometimes, when young people make a mistake, they feel unlovable or unworthy of respect. These feelings can get in the way of dealing with mistakes, learning from them, and moving on. Clear the path of those feelings of doubt.

One of the most important things we can do to help kids is model a healthy attitude toward our own mistakes. Don't let children see you beat yourself up over mistakes. Instead, when you make a mistake, point it out to kids and show them how you own it, fix it, and learn from it. Praise others who you notice doing the same. It can even be helpful—and fun—to intentionally make mistakes in front of the group and then talk about them. Tell stories about your life—moments when you failed, bounced back, and ultimately succeeded because of a mistake you made. Positive role models can make a lasting impression on kids.

Learning how to deal with mistakes takes time. It's an ongoing process. But in most cases, our assurances, feedback, and guidance will eventually help kids get better at handling mistakes.

However, if your child or student continues to deny mistakes or crumble under the weight of them, consider finding or recommending professional help. The school guidance counselor is a good resource. So is Mental Health America. Their website (mentalhealthamerica.net) includes links to finding mental health professionals in your area.

Resources for Kids

Your Fantastic Elastic Brain: Stretch It, Shape It by JoAnn Deak, Ph.D., Little Pickle Press, 2010.

Mistakes That Worked: 40 Familiar Inventions & How They Came to Be by Charlotte Foltz Jones, Delacorte Press, 1991.

What to Do When Mistakes Make You Quake: A Kid's Guide to Accepting Imperfection by Claire A. B. Freeland, Ph.D., and Jacqueline B. Toner, Ph.D., Magination Press, 2016.

"Saying You're Sorry," KidsHealth.org, kidshealth.org/en/kids/sorry.html.

What to Do When Good Enough Isn't Good Enough by Thomas S. Greenspon, Ph.D., Free Spirit Publishing, 2007.

Index

About the Authors and Illustrator

Kimberly Feltes Taylor has written over 15 books for young people, including the popular Yolanda series of advice books, which provide tips for dealing with peer pressure, family issues, friendship problems, money management, and workplace dilemmas. Kim has also written dozens of classroom magazine articles. She lives in the Twin Cities of Minnesota.

Eric Braun is a super-rad world-famous combination pro skateboarder and rock star. Oh, wait—that's a mistake. Actually Eric is the author of dozens of books for kids and teens on many topics including sports, money smarts, wilderness survival, and fractured fairy tales. Whenever he makes a mistake, which is often, you will see him pumping his fist and going "YES!" because he knows he is learning and growing. He lives in Minneapolis with his wife, two sons, and a dog named Willis whom he never forgets to walk.

Steve Mark is a freelance illustrator and a part-time puppeteer. He lives in Minnesota and is the father of three and the husband of one. Steve has illustrated all the books in the Laugh & Learn series, including *Don't Behave Like You Live in a Cave* and *Bullying Is a Pain in the Brain*.

Free Spirit's
Laugh & Learn® Series

Solid information, a kid-centric point of view, and a sense of humor combine to make each book in our Laugh & Learn series an invaluable tool for getting through life's rough spots. For ages 8–13. *Paperback; 80–128 pp.; illust.; 5⅛" x 7"*